A Guide To:

Learning
To
Live
Or
Die
Comfortably

Terri Kerscher

Copyright © 2021 Terri Kerscher

ALL RIGHTS RESERVED. No part of this book may be reproduced by any mechanical, photographic or electronic process, or in the form of a phonographic recording; nor may it be stored in a retrieval system, transmitted, or otherwise be copied for public or private use – other than for "fair use" as brief quotations embodied in articles and reviews-without prior written permission of the publisher.

The author of this does not dispense medical advice or prescribe the use of any technique as a form of treatment for physical, emotional or medical problems without the advice of a physician, whether directly or indirectly. In the event you use any of the information in this book for yourself, the author and the publisher assume no responsibility for your actions.

Forward:

I had the honor of being taught by this "Collective" of Arch Angels. As I typed this book, I learned new information and processes. This has been a very rewarding experience that I have loved doing! Who knew I would work with angels and type a book for them? I am so thankful they chose me to help them as I also got to spend time with them and their unconditional love.

Dedication:

This book of love is dedicated to the Arch Angels that channeled it to me.
And to my wonderful family for the love and acceptance they have always given me

Table of Contents

Forward: 3
Dedication 3
Introduction: 5
Feeling Energy 8
Talking with Spirit 11
Uglies and Negative Removal 16
Practicing Feeling Energy 19
Processes to Help People 26
Changes and Choices in My Life 31
More Helping Processes 33
Few More Things 41
About the Author 43

Introduction:

The goal of this book is to teach people to feel energy and live comfortably with it, so they can live their lives in love and joy!

This is Terri, you will see as you read this book, it was channeled to me from a collective of Arch Angels. They will speak as a Collective unless one of them feels the need to explain something that has to do with their specialty. The AA that you see is a reference to Arch Angel and the initials will be for the individual Arch Angel. We will spell them out in this Introduction, then they will be initials. As you read through this book, some of the information is directed to me, as I channel them and I ask questions on occasion and/or respond to some things that they say.

AAMI (Michael): This will be the beginning of the book. You will write to explain to others how to help people work through their issues when it gets closer to the time for them to pass. Sometimes you will be working with people who have no higher power and we will help you with explanations that will help them to get through it and you will mostly be working with people who do have a higher power but don't know how to work through their issues.

AAA (Azrael): My job is to help people pass over when it is time to come home to the energetic portion of themselves that will be waiting for them.

AAG (Gabriel): My job is to help you find the best words and ways to communicate with the people you are trying to help.

AAJ (Jophiel) My job is to help you show people the way to fix their issues so they can move on to hospice and to passing and to teach people the joy of living while they are alive.

AAMe (Metatron): My job is to make it logical so you can understand what we are telling you and how to get it done in the most logical manner.

AAR (Raphael): My job is to help people with physical, emotional and spiritual issues so they can be helped and healed before they move to the next step of their life path to live their lives or which could be hospice if they are ill.

AAU (Uriel): My job to help you in any way I can, especially in removing dark, shadowy or ugly things from people and making their transition to hospice much easier and kinder.

This is the first time we have taught this "program" to anyone and we are grateful that Terri stepped up to be the one to work it first. She naturally draws people to herself and they are instantly comfortable because of her demeanor and light. It will also be easier to bring people to her to learn how to do this after we have helped her put this book and class together. In the meantime, we will help her in any way that we can. She also has the Creators, Jesus, Mother Mary, Kuan Yin, her Reiki Masters and Native family to help with the healing in any way they can! This is an exciting thing we do and we are planning on enjoying it with Terri, every step of the way!

Feeling Energy

As you do this you will need to continue to pay more attention to how the room feels when you enter, or how the office is when you get to work, or how the person next to you feels as you stand in a line. You have blocked yourself for so many years because it is so overwhelming that you need to relearn how to do this. We will keep it from overwhelming you while you do practice and also teach you how to block energy more effectively while you learn.

Q: How do I keep from picking up every dark/negative/ugly in this century if I have my walls down? C: We will teach you to place a shield against negative energy around you that will still allow you to feel what is outside of your aura but not come in. T: That will be an absolute bonus to learn that! It will help so many people too! C: Yes, it will! T: I love this and being able to share it too~

C: Sit with your eyes closed and visualize (or as close as you can get to visualizing) someone's energy coming in, now pause and identify the feeling that you are feeling... frustrating is what I'm getting. Ok, now you can release it out of your aura. Next time you go to town or the neighbors or anywhere, don't open up to everyone and their individual energy, just the overall energy of the building or room. If it's negative, use a thought to clean it, then fill it with love and light. If it's joyous, enjoy it. It will become second nature to do these things after you practice. T: Ok! Thanks! I'll practice it!

You have a gatekeeper when it comes to the dead so you are not swamped and overwhelmed. They have to wait until you are ready to hear them or you call someone to you to help, whether it's to go to the light or for a message. This is another place you need to pay better attention to or start having your gatekeeper start telling you that you have people who need help. Some will have messages for their loved ones and others are just lost and need to go to the light. You actually won't do a lot of this because you are going to be so busy helping people fix themselves. This is what normal mediums do every day and it would behoove you to know how they do it. Then it will be easier for you to understand when you do start talking to people's angels and guides to help them heal from their fears and misconceptions. This will also help your healing practice with the ongoing and living people. You do a certain amount of this now but you will need to do a lot more. You can do this randomly to practice. It's not intrusive if you aren't doing anything with it, just connecting to say hi!

Talking with Spirit

People have beliefs that aren't always for their greatest and highest good and they don't even know it. This so true of so many people. Religion has not helped when they have used fear to keep people in line down the centuries instead of letting them be who they are and talk to Creator themselves, like we all can. As you learn to do this it will prove to be a challenge in many ways, but as you learn the best ways to help people regardless of who they are and what they think, it will become easier and you will find yourself having more finesse doing this and having even more love to share. You will get tired some days and other times it will lift you up beyond the heavens! You do need to get in better shape so you will have the stamina to do this for the thousands of people who need it!

You will actually be talking to a person's higher self, angels or guides, whichever is willing to help and can direct your traffic to the issues that need dealt with. There will be some horrific stuff you will hear about and you will need to learn to be very objective and we will provide dialogue to help work through it as you go. All the healers you have will also help you. You do need to take time to get to know your Reiki healers and Native family better so you can call them by name and get it right. T: Ok, I certainly will!

You already know that a medium, talks to dead people, either those that never went to the light or to those that have come back and want a message given to their families or someone they are worried and/or care about. You will talk to some dead people about what you are going to do to help people get ready to pass but not as much as their spirit crew.

Let's practice some spirit work. T: I shut down so much that I knew because it was overwhelming and I currently don't identify different energies very easily or well. How do I start identifying who it is? C: By the feel of it and if that never works, they will just have to say who they are. They will have to say who they are anyway until you can feel the difference. T: OK. Let's practice!

T: Well, it worked ok for the most part. I still need to identify Rafael and Uriel for sure, I could get everyone else. I'll just keep practicing! I got the idea that color might work but I won't always have my eyes closed but I still like the idea of identifying them with color, crystals and feel, just so I know for sure it's them!

C: Are you ready to practice again? T: Yes, I am. Can we type for a bit since I'm sitting and ready? C: Of course.

One of the things you will need to know is that not every one's angels or Spirit guides are going to want to talk to you since they don't know you. Our suggestion as you start to work with someone is to take a moment, introduce yourself to them verbally and then mentally and listen to what they have to say. Most of them will be ready and already know you are coming, but some will want to make sure you are who they are waiting for. T: So how do I identify myself in a way that will help them to recognize me?

C: By your energy. Since you will be having Arch Angels, guides, etc.... help you, your vibration is high and will be higher because of us and we will help identify you too when it's needed. Your biggest challenge will be people who don't believe in a higher power or in heaven and are afraid to die because they may believe in hell or just nothing and are fearful, they will be nothing after they die. We need to help write up some dialogue that will help these people that you can use. The ones who believe in God are a lot easier but as you know with your mom, they are not always willing to hear what you have to say because they aren't sure they believe in heaven or something like heaven. Sadly, a lot of God believers are also Devil believers so they expect to go to hell and that is actually what will meet them because it's what they are expecting. It won't stay that way because there actually is no hell, but whatever they expect to see is what everyone gets! You believe in angels and crystal buildings... that's what you get. It is whatever you want, you create whatever you want.

For this to work you will need to work on your ability to talk to anyone's angels and to be comfortable with any type person you come in contact with. The largest amount of people you work with will be older and they can be very cranky and bullheaded. Gaining their trust is going to be an interesting road to walk but you instinctively know how to do this with people so it will be easier for you than most. Holding their hand while you talk to them will be #1 on your list. That way your crew can talk to their crew and see what kind of help they need to release any thing that will be holding them back from moving to hospice when it's their time to move on. Or they may never go to hospice and still need the help to release their issues and pass on.

This is going to be a very rewarding job when you get it all laid out and doing what it's meant to do! You will be well known! T: You know that's not important to me, unless it will allow me to help even more people than I can without being well known. C: It will! Believe us, it will! T: Ok. That should shock more than a few people that know me! LOL! C: Do you care if it does shock them? T: Nope, I don't!

Uglies and Negative Removal

While you are thinking about it, you will need to remove more than your fair share of entities and uglies while you are doing this. Your spirit guides and us angels will help just like they always have and you can do it smoothly and keep moving. You will need to ask God if it's ok to remove them if you cannot get their permission, but 99.9% of the time it will be fine. Like you were told after your mom passed, you can always ask God for permission to remove entities from someone. If it is for the persons higher good, permission will be granted and AAMI and his band have agreed to continue to help with that. You will have to work your processes for each one to be done in your head and not out loud because most people will not be comfortable with what you are doing.

T: Question- If God agrees to me removing dark entities and I take them out, will their persons angels/guides keep replacing the light for the person if they start to slip back into the dark behavior if we haven't told them what I am doing? C: Yes, they will. Their angels/guides always want what is best for them, just like yours do, they will step up to help! T: Thank you!

T: While I am holding their hands, will I be able to still read them but not get uglies on /in me because my light will attract them and I will be holding their hands? C: Yes, we will teach you how. T: Ok. If I start cleaning someone before I go see them, will that remove the uglies from the person I am going to see before I go? C: Yes, you can and it would probably be the best way to do it actually. You may not have time with some people but either way will be efficient. Good thought! T: Thank you!

As you start to learn how to do this you need to remember that regardless of what happens, that is what is supposed to be happening. Just so you know there will be people that you help and will die a day or two later or a week later or may try to pass as you are working on them. When they are older and have been sick and in pain, then you help them, help themselves and provide the clearing that they need, that will be exactly what they have been waiting for and may never make it to hospice care because they don't or won't need that last step. Pain and age are hard things to live with and it can change people's whole demeanor and personality. This will be challenging as you first start, until you get some practice and put it all together. After that it will be much smoother and easier on you and even easier on the people you work on. Yes, you will be doing some of the same work on people not even close to dying because of their age, good health, etc... It will be part of what helps them to awaken, heal themselves and live the rest of their lives following their path that they created with God/Creator. The joy that will bring to each of them will be amazing and a joyful sight to see!

T: Great! Thank you!

Practicing Feeling Energy

You have now met all your angels and guides and still need to spend time with each of them so that you have intimate knowledge of them and how they can help you with this endeavor of a new modality. T: Yes, I do need to do that. I will make a goal of talking to one each day and learning about them individually so I can put the whole of their knowledge together to make this work! Thank you! I think I will start with the Arch Angels and do Azreal today if that's ok? Azreal are you up for this? AAA: Yes of course!

T: What can you tell me about you that I will need to know to do my job? AA Azreal: I am the Arch Angel of grieving and/or dying people. I help them survive their grief when someone dies and I help them to come to terms with their loss. I also help people who are ill and getting ready to pass, I help them accept who they are and what they have done in their life so they can relax and let themselves go to heaven when the time comes. Like what you are going to do with a lot of people too. You have the perfect personality to do this with people. You are kind, loving, accepting and joyous and people who have troubles accepting who they are and what they have done will love your acceptance as you teach them to accept themselves and Gods' love! I do help healers, helpers and counselors as they help people help themselves. Ask me for assistance contacting dead people. I can cover you in white light to help you too! It is my color. T: Thank you so much! I will love working with you!

T: How about AA Gabriel now? Are you ready for this today? AAG: Of course! I am the Arch Angel that helps people when they are working on learning new knowledge about themselves and others, I also help new mothers as they become pregnant, have their babies and raise them. I help all people with their need to be creative and figure out what they can do to create what is in their souls.... I will help you and all the others to figure out this new process that you will be learning and the best way to do the steps to make it work for everyone. There will need to be a couple of different ways depending on whether they believe in God/Creator or not. This will be such a joy to be a part of this process to help so many people find the help that they need to transition to heaven or to just live their lives in the highest and best way for each of them as they walk their paths.

This is so tiring because you are a pure channel and that helps us more than you will ever know, however, using/being energy in this way does take a lot of your energy to stay open and keep listening without losing focus, needing to get up and walk or just needing to stop. The vibration difference is part of what makes it so tiring too. You have a really high vibration but not as high as ours yet, so yours has to go up exponentially and ours has to lower. Thank goodness you have had the DNA changes that allows this to be done and not burn you out. You have wondered, haven't you? T: Yes, I did! Thanks for the confirmation!

AA Jeremiel are you ready? ~ Yes, I am, thank you! I work with the dead to help them pass over and to being comfortable and recognizing that everyone dies and that they will go to heaven and be fine. Their spirit is eternal and not everyone really believes that. It will be one of your hardest lessons to get people to believe. I will help teach you how to talk to people so they are comfortable and to explain how heaven works for their spirit as it leaves them. They are rather startled when they realize that leaving their body is a pulling sensation and a popping noise as it comes lose from their body. When they are out of their body they are confused and it takes them time to really understand that they are done and can move on to the light. I will help you help them! T: Thank you!

AA Metatron, are you ready? ~ Yes, I am! Nice to talk to you again! T: Thank you, nice to talk to you again too! ~My job is to help people understand the logistics of dying and exactly how it works and where they go. AAJ and I work together on this one. My whole existence has been to help people understand the workings of the universe and how it pertains to them. Helping them learn to pass on will be a joy so that they can come home and be with the rest of their energy and with God again!

AA Michael: Your turn! AAMi: Thank you! By the way it is a joy to work with you every day and do the things we do together. You worry that doing the same things over and over every day will be boring for me but it's not. I'm just glad to hang out with you and be able to help you! T: Thank you! I love working with you too and appreciate your help and understanding more than you will ever know! AAMi: My job will be to help people pass over too. I can lead them to the light or wait on the other side for them. I can help people who are passing over and those that have passed and not gone to the light, to get there now. You have always been a big help with those that need to pass through the light whether they have just died or been wandering for years. You are a natural! T: Thank you! It's nice to hear that I'm doing it right. AAMi: You just need to ask us all more questions and let us help you with the issues you have come up. We won't make your decisions for you but we will let you know about something that will hurt you. T: Thank you! I will do more of that!

AA Raphael: Are you ready? AAR: Yes, I am! Thank you! My job is to help your healing flow easier and to add my own to it so it works as well as it needs to work. You do such a clean and good job of getting the Universal energy into and around the people that need it that you make my job a lot easier! T: Thank you! AAR: You are welcome! Just telling the truth! You also have the others that help you and overall, it works well and efficiently! I can also help direct people to you and to help you find words to help them. We have some fabulous word smiths in this group so you won't be failing for words to say! I can use my colored healing energy on whoever needs it to heal and whoever needs it to pass. There is always a color, vibration and healing for whoever needs it.

AA Uriel; T: Are you ready? AAU: Yes, I am too, thank you! My job is to help you remove emotions and energies from people that does not serve their highest good! I will help you remove the things that you remove from people and send them to the light so no one else is distressed by them. I will also help you find the words to help you explain to people what is happening to them as you hold their hands and talk to their angels at the same time. Good thing you can do two things at once, you will need that ability a lot!

So now that you are through the angels and their purposes in helping you, you will need to continue to talk and visit with each of them so you are more comfortable with the newer ones, versus your old friends that you have been working with for years!

You are finding yourself getting ready to do a lot of different things right now and that's good. It will make it easier to do it all at once than to have one change, then another and another.... Get a job, house, business and new modality all at once. Then you can settle down and enjoy doing what you need to do, to walk your path a bit more solidly.

At this time, you will be living somewhere you weren't planning on but that won't be forever, and for now it will work. As long as you can hang out and get to know the manager you will make some other really good friends in the complex and gain a lot of business from there. So, do that for now!

You did a good job on your journey today! And don't worry so much about what others think will happen in your life. Pay attention to what it feels like to have the things that you want in your life because you want them and you deserve them! You do need a vision board of one form or another!

Processes to Help People

When you approach people and they want your services, make sure you clarify what it is that they need and want. The elderly sometimes won't know what they need as you know, but the knowledge that you care about them and like to spend time with them will make a big difference in how close you can get to them and what you can do to help them will be appreciated. There will be a lot of times that the elderly won't really know why you are there if their family has hired you to help them get comfortable so they can do what they need to do, whether that is to pass or to live on and be happy. You will be surprised at the amount of people that will come to you first only to discover that you can help their parents and grandparents. You can take yourself to where ever they are and help them in the comfort of their own homes or facilities.

Now it's time to write down some of the processes that you will need to do to help people.

Start out with introductions and explanations of who and what you are and can accomplish for them. As you go on you will learn what exactly you need to do to help each person that you work on because their angels and all of us will help you hear what needs to be done and hear how best to solve it.

Ask how you can help them, what they expect and if they understand what Reiki is. You might explain that you are also a Clinical Hypnotherapist and how that works and explain that when you use the two of them together it makes it easier to understand the best way that you can help them by asking them certain questions and helping them to understand what needs to be taken care of to give them new choices, changes or a new more positive way of life.

A good explanation of Reiki is when you had the attunements from a certified teacher who had also had them, it allowed your body to be cleaned out energetically and allows the energy (which is God's energy) to flow through the top of your head and come out the palms of your hands. At which time you can either place your hand with appropriate permissions on their body or to be ran above the top of their body so they can feel the energy come out of your hands. You can also volunteer to hold hands with them to see if they can feel it, not everyone can feel Reiki energy, but some can.

While you are in contact with them as you visit, have your guides or angels introduce you to their guides or angels and see what kind of issues they need help with, especially if they are not sure themselves.

The thing that you need to know now is that this is something that will help you and everyone you come in contact with throughout the rest of your life! The more people that you can touch and talk to, the more that will be started down this path to their best life. Just like you are doing.

As you visit with the person ask them how you can help them. If they don't know for sure, ask them if they have any regrets or things that they wish they could change about things that have happened in their lives. Discuss these life happenings with them and ask them what they wish they would have done differently. This is where you can go to their angels and help clean those things out and give them a clean start for the end if they are older and /or will give them a new start where ever they are in their lifetime and to live the rest of their lives in peace and light and joy without the regrets.

When you can hold hands with people that is an easy way to connect with them and their angels. The physical contact is just a natural connection and people appreciate the attention and the physical contact with someone else, just like you do!

When you start talking to your angels and they start talking to the person you are with, remember to pay attention to the feel of their energy and the feel of their sorrows too. You will be able to tell if they have entities attached or if the sorrows are just regular and have become an issue for them through repetition. You know you can ask God if you can remove them without the persons permission because they are not in the persons highest good. So that is another way to help them too. There are just so many ways to help people with what you are starting to do! It's so exciting!

You can always combine your Reiki and your Hypnotherapy like you have already and use it all that way. You can have them help you by looking for the lack of light in themselves while you are actually teaching them to scan themselves and can do it any time they need to. Then you teach them to call on AAMI and get him to help them remove what is not in their highest good and to pull their cords, roots and seeds and then fill them with golden and white shiny light from God! Just like you do to yourself a couple of times a day. By removing those connections that are not good for them it teaches them how they can feel good and lighter and they have done it with an angel's help. Most will love that!

You can always do what A did with Hypnotherapy and the wall (block) that needs to be taken down and removed. We will work out a way to do that in your Reiki sessions if they are opposed to doing hypnotherapy. It can all be done for their highest good with the tools you have and the ones that will continue to come to the surface and you will learn to use. You will enjoy the Karuna Reiki class you are going to take! It will be an eye opener and also teach you how to give a class yourself so you can learn to do them too. You will love that! You are a natural born teacher and you make it fun! Most people who hang with you learn what you know and do, because you talk of them so easily and with so much enjoyment! Then they are intrigued and want to know more, so you are always there to help them learn to help themselves!

Changes and Choices in My Life

This is a scary time but if you stay in and stay safe it will all be fine! We realize that you are not scared but if you were, you just have to follow the guidelines and do what you are being told. We won't go over them all again now because you don't need them in this book.

So, the teaching thing for you will be a good bonus when it comes. You are having some questions about starting your own business or getting a part time job and doing your healing in the evenings. Either way is fine, but you do need to get yourself going in that direction. Call on the buildings you saw on 17th and ask them what they charge. We will help you make up your mind to what will work best for you. We are tickled for you to have a place of your own. When you get there, you can create your own schedule and do whatever works for you food wise, time wise, prayer wise. Whatever, it will be your decision. And yes, as you know from your journaling this morning you lived with your friends long enough to be ok with an apartment for now and then you will move on to a house that you want. It is all in place and just waiting for the vibrations to match and to come forward for you. It also is depending on a couple of other people that are considering what they want to do. It will be to your advantage when the time comes. So, relax, keep your whole life with God and you just keep doing what needs to be done. Yes, you can still put in for jobs but the one you want will be along in a couple of months and will be perfect for you if you still want it. *Ok, Thank you so much! Been fussing about these things and I appreciate you letting me know!

You have had some interesting experiences this week with K and we are glad you had them. Those are things you needed to learn and you enjoyed learning from a person instead of a book. So good for you! You will need to type up all that information from her, and you already know that, but put those parts in sections by themselves so you can copy and paste them in other places for you to use. You may add it all to this book. We aren't sure yet. It will be whatever works.

More Helping Processes

So on to learning more. You will need to practice on people that don't mind you talking to their angels and you will have to make it quiet and internal like what you did with your friend when you cleaned her cords and uglies off! It will take focus and we realize that sometimes focusing is hard for you. So, we will help by reminding you and to help you find rituals that will work better for you and be easy to remember and able to shortcut anything too long. It will make it pleasant for whoever you are working on.

When you talk to the angels, you will have needed to talk to the person first and just visit with them and get to know them so you can get to know the questions to ask for any regrets or sorrows or hurts that need released so they can be comfortable passing when their time comes. When we started talking to you about this you automatically thought it would be mostly about working with old people so they could pass, as time has passed, we have noticed that you will work with older people but you will also work with middle aged and younger too so they can live their lives without the regrets, sorrows or hurts that they carry already. With luck they will learn from you how to change the way they think or process emotions so you can help them not gather up any more regrets, sorrows or hurts in their lives and live a happy and loving life until they die.

You have had a busy week and interesting life at this point! Don't get discouraged if it takes you a bit to get moved in to your new apartment. You may have a week or two that you can spend putting things away that you have brought from Blackfoot to IF and then bring in the bigger stuff after that. Ask J if you can use her truck, she will let you! You still need to take care of your anger problem with yourself and do a few other things, so when you can get that done so you can move on sooner!

While you are working with people you will need to really pay attention to how they are feeling emotionally and physically. As you know, emotions will manifest in the physical body and the emotional of course. You need to find a way to ease them into telling you what they are feeling in all the ways and then work with them on going through their issues. Ask them what bothers them the most and go from there.

When you discuss issues with their angels be sure you take notes and keep track of what is being said and what else you may need to do. Practice on P while you are here, she'll get a kick out of it! *Question: when I am talking to her angels, do I talk to them or let my angels talk to them and they tell me. That seems to be how I have always done it up to now. Is that correct? ~Actually yes, for you. Others would take a more direct path and you can too, but it's not necessary if you don't want to... As long at the message is clear and concise either way is fine. *Ok, thank you!

When you put your hands on someone, as you know, your Reiki instantly comes on and you have no control over it, it just happens. You don't have to worry about getting permission to run it on someone, everyone can use the energy if their subconscious accepts it and you don't really get to vote whether someone gets it or not, so let it go....

So now it's time to discuss how everyone can help themselves while you are helping them. You need to explain that they are a free agent and because of that they have free will. With free will comes the ability to believe these things we are going to tell you or not. You, as you know, cannot heal anyone. All you are is the conduit that the Universal energy goes through and the person you are directing it at, is the person with the option to accept it or not. They also cannot choose where this energy goes as it will go to their highest and greatest good! Which means, where ever our body needs it the most at this time. What everyone who accepts healing needs to do is come to the realization that their body can and will heal itself if you give it the correct tools. By which we mean feed their body correctly with good food, get some exercise, meditate or do something your soul loves, practice being kind to themselves and others and connect with a higher power regardless what they call it. You need life balance and selflove for each of you to walk your life paths and learn to love yourself and others without judgement, to learn to accept others for who they are and what they are capable of doing, of realizing that your reality and someone else's are not always the same because of the different ways you were raised, with different ideas and tenants from your parents and those around you. And love them all with their differences and because of them. If, however, you find people that are polar opposites of you and what you believe in, you will need to still practice acceptance and love and leave them alone to be who they are....

Practicing acceptance and love are very hard things for humans to do because they were mostly raised to believe that their religion or life styles are the best way to live and anything else is wrong or not as it should be, so everyone should just step up and believe and live like they do. For those of you who see that life is different from what you have been taught and that there are other options, good for you! It means you have an open mind and are willing to learn a different and possibly better way which will make your life here on Earth a much easier place for you to be in!

As you go along on your path you will come to many forks and lots of different options and at these times you need to stop and listen to your body and what it is telling you. Your intuition is one of the most wonderful things you have to direct you toward doing what is best for you! As you stop and ask yourself which option is best for you, road 1 or road 2, stop with each option and see what reaction your get from your body. If you get a tingling/pleasant/good feeling in your gut that means you need to do which ever option you were thinking about at the time. If you get an unpleasant/sharp/icky feeling in your gut then don't do that one! (Terri has ignored her instincts more than once and was very sad she did when she had to experience those choices and they hurt her.) You can also muscle test to help you decide what is best for you. To muscle test you need to stand up straight, make your knees soft and place your hands on/at heart level and then ask your body (with only those parts that are for your highest and greatest good and in the light) whether (you fill in the blank) is true or not. Some people will sway to the front for a yes and backwards for a no or it can be the opposite. Then ask it if your name is what it really is and watch your reaction to that. Which direction you sway according to what is a yes answer or a no is your pattern to use this method on everything else, such as "should I eat this" or "do I need this vitamin" or "should I buy this"? Any question you have can be answered this way. After a while you may be able to just know what is right or wrong for you because you have checked in enough with your body to know whether you need it or not by how your body feels.

You all need to connect with Mother Earth and work on being grounded. Some people can meditate and be grounded, some people need to visualize being grounded through their feet and others just think it and it's done. In your area of Idaho Falls, there is dirt, lava and then clay. You can visualize your feet growing tendrils/roots and they are going into the earth, as they go through the dirt they will come to the lava and will have to find ways around and through the lava openings, when they get to the clay you will feel the wonderful energy of Mother Earth as it comes up through your feet, into your legs and up your body to eventually come out your crown to rain down into your aura and back in Mother Earth. If you have been ungrounded, you will be amazed at how wonderful and how focused you will feel. It will help you have clarity too!

There are very different gifts that God/Creator/Universal Oneness, etc., has given each of you to help you along your life paths. Some of you know intuitively how someone feels or you may suddenly have a pain somewhere and when you ask yourself you realize it's not yours and you can send it away. You may be able to see spirits or hear them, or naturally do hands on healing or have chosen to do one of the Reiki modalities to help people heal. Some people use music as their gift to help people work through issues or to relax. Everything that you are, you have, you think or even breath is universal energy and it is all vibration. Some people combine sound and color to help someone clean their aura field and chakras with the vibrations of both. The energy world is a varying and complex place with a lot of options that are open to anyone who chooses to learn new ways of thought and new ways of doing things. Open your mind to the wisdom and knowledge that is out there for you to use on yourself to selfheal or to use on others to help them heal themselves.

Everyone has different issues that they need help with and you would be amazed by the help that energy work can do for you to help you overcome fears, phobias, self-esteem issues, anger issues, depression, anxiety and lots of others too. With everyone having different realities and thought processes it sometimes seems like there are no places to start or it's too hard to find one when you're new to the energy world. Ask people you trust if they know someone, they are comfortable with that can help them with their issues. Someone always knows someone else who knows someone else that can help. Don't give up, if you do find someone that you're not really comfortable with, don't stay, but don't quit looking, there is someone out there for you to work with, that will help you open yourself up and start moving your vibration up too. It's a matter of waking up in these new times with Mother Earth going from a 3D world to a 5D world and you will need to start working on that transition.

Few More Things

There are only a few more things that we want to you put in this book. We could go on and on forever about the things we want people to know, but right now this will suffice to begin.

Terri, you do a good job with your morning ritual of thanking the Creators of the Universe for your life and every day that you are on this earth and have the opportunity to learn the lessons that you came to learn and to help all the people that you meet. Sometimes we don't think that you realize that you help each and every person that you talk to or interact with. Your energy is such that it automatically shares itself with whoever you are interacting with and feeds their energy level and attitude, which is always brighter after you have talked to someone. Because you like people so well and interact with them on such a loving level, you have spent your whole life helping them and not even realizing it! We have always loved that you do this! *Thank you! I didn't realize I did that every time!

You will notice that when you meet someone, new or known, your aura lights up and you shine more at that second. If you hug them and/or are really glad to see them, it gets even brighter still. That's why so many small children will look at you because you radiate love and light and they are attracted to it. You have noticed how many smaller children follow you with their eyes even across spaces. *Yes, I have noticed that! I like it! ~You should! It's a good and positive thing to have happen.

About the Author

Terri loves doing energy work and started down this Spiritual and Metaphysical path about 8 years ago when she lived in Arizona. She currently lives in Idaho Falls, Idaho and is the owner of Celestial Wellness Center, Inc. Terri's accomplishments include Usui Reiki® Master, Holy Fire® III Karuna Reiki® Master, Clinical Hypnotherapist, and a Minister of the Universal Life Church.

Using Reiki or Hypnotherapy which are offered through The Celestial Wellness Center will help people relax, sleep better, bring comfort during challenging times with peace and love and to resolve issues they may have learning to love themselves. Using her Crystal Singing Bowls, Terri will balance your Chakra energies and teach you to heal yourself.

Terri also offers "Distance Reiki®" over the phone and internet to help clients stay safe during these challenging times.

Through the guidance of your angels and information learned from this book, each will help you learn to live your life in the happiest and most loving manner possible.

Thank you for reading this book, we all hope it has helped you! To contact Terri please email her at: cwcpeace@gmail.com.

www.ingramcontent.com/pod-product-compliance
Lightning Source LLC
Chambersburg PA
CBHW070042070426
42449CB00012BA/3139